40
DAYS

LUKE

Scripture Union England & Wales
Trinity House, Opal Court, Fox Milne, Milton Keynes, MK15 0DF
info@scriptureunion.org.uk
www.scriptureunion.org.uk

40 Days uses Scripture quotations taken from The Holy Bible, New International Version (Anglicised edition). Copyright © 1979, 1984, 2011 by Biblica. Used by permission of Hodder & Stoughton Publishers, a Hachette UK company. All rights reserved.

This content has been adapted from material that first appeared in *Closer to God* 2011–2015 (SU).

With thanks to the writers: Phil Andrews, Tricia Marnham, Rebekah Callow, Lizzie Telfer, Esther Youlten, Phil Caroe, Martin Hodson, Richard England, Luke Davydaitis, Helen Paynter, Elaine Carr, Penny Boshoff

Design: Max Randall
Layout: Lizzie Evans
Editor: Caleb Woodbridge

Printed and bound in India by Thomson Press India Ltd

 Scripture Union is an international Christian charity working with churches in more than 130 countries.

Thank you for purchasing this book. Any profits from this book support SU in England and Wales to bring the good news of Jesus Christ to children, young people and families and to enable them to meet God through the Bible and prayer.

Find out more about our work and how you can get involved at:
www.scriptureunion.org.uk (England and Wales)
www.suscotland.org.uk (Scotland)
www.suni.co.uk (Northern Ireland)
www.scriptureunion.org (USA)
www.su.org.au (Australia)

Welcome...

40 days isn't very long. But it's long enough to take a journey through Luke's Gospel while taking some time out to reflect, think and pray.

Luke tells us that in writing his Gospel he 'carefully investigated everything from the beginning... so that you may know the certainty of the things you have been taught' (1:3,4). He includes many details of Jesus' life and teaching that we get nowhere else, including his childhood time in the Temple, the parable of the Prodigal Son (or sons), and the encounter on the road to Emmaus.

Through Luke's account, we see Jesus' passion for the poor, and ministry in the power of the Holy Spirit. Jesus spends time with people from all levels of society: from proud Pharisees to rich tax-collectors to outcast widows. He is both Israel's promised King, come to the Jews at last, and the Saviour of Gentiles who sends his disciples to all nations.

Come and spend time with Jesus. Prepare to be amazed, baffled, challenged and delighted by him as you encounter him through his Word. Talk to him, listen to him, and discover again the wonder of who he is and all he has done for you.

Caleb Woodbridge

How to use this book

This book contains 40 excerpts from Luke's Gospel, with plenty of space to help you reflect on, engage with and apply what you have read. If you have a Bible, you might want to read the book of Luke from beginning to end – there's a lot more than we could include here and it will give you a fuller picture of Jesus' life and teachings.

Before you start reading, **take time to be quiet** and ask God to speak to you. Ask the Holy Spirit to bring the words to life.

Get into the Bible... Read the passage. What's the main point? What is God showing me about himself or about my life? Use the suggestions or questions to prompt reflection.

We have deliberately given you the space to ask big questions and to grapple honestly with God in prayer. Grab a pen to jot down thoughts or to underline words or phrases that stand out to you. There is plenty of space to **respond** to what God has shown you through journaling or prayer suggestions. You'll also find a number of questions and comments to consider along the way.

As you start this book, you might want to pray that the Holy Spirit will bring Luke's Gospel to life, and that through these words you will get to know Jesus in a fresh and life-changing way.

¹ Many have undertaken to draw up an account of the things that have been fulfilled among us, ² just as they were handed down to us by those who from the first were eyewitnesses and servants of the word. ³ With this in mind, since I myself have carefully investigated everything from the beginning, I too decided to write an orderly account for you, most excellent Theophilus, ⁴ so that you may know the certainty of the things you have been taught.

Luke 1:1–4

Day 1

Luke wants Theophilus to be sure of what he has been taught about Jesus. What do you already know about Jesus? Write down some of your thoughts.

. . . .

. . . .

. . . .

. . . .

. . . .

. . . .

. . . .

. . . .

. . . .

. . . .

. . . .

Luke 'investigated everything from the beginning' (v 3). As you prepare to journal through Luke's Gospel, pray for fresh eyes and an open heart to receive the hope it offers us.

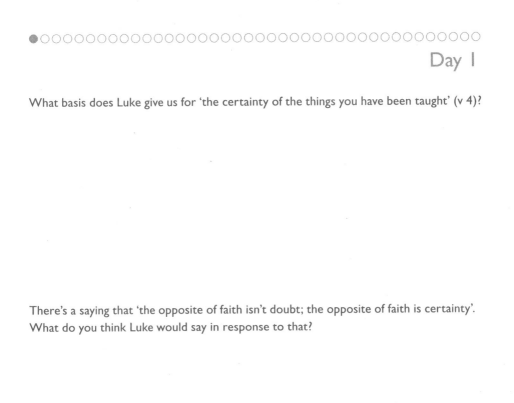

What basis does Luke give us for 'the certainty of the things you have been taught' (v 4)?

There's a saying that 'the opposite of faith isn't doubt; the opposite of faith is certainty'. What do you think Luke would say in response to that?

Ask God to be at work, through his Holy Spirit, in deepening your certainty about Jesus' life, identity and ministry.

Day 2

26 In the sixth month of Elizabeth's pregnancy, God sent the angel Gabriel to Nazareth, a town in Galilee, 27 to a virgin pledged to be married to a man named Joseph, a descendant of David. The virgin's name was Mary.
28 The angel went to her and said, 'Greetings, you who are highly favoured! The Lord is with you.'
29 Mary was greatly troubled at his words and wondered what kind of greeting this might be. 30 But the angel said to her, 'Do not be afraid, Mary, you have found favour with God. 31 You will conceive and give birth to a son, and you are to call him Jesus. 32 He will be great and will be called the Son of the Most High. The Lord God will give him the throne of his father David, 33 and he will reign over Jacob's descendants for ever; his kingdom will never end.'
34 'How will this be,' Mary asked the angel, 'since I am a virgin?'
35 The angel answered, 'The Holy Spirit will come on you, and the power of the Most High will overshadow you. So the holy one to be born will be called the Son of God.
36 Even Elizabeth your relative is going to have a child in her old age, and she who was said to be unable to conceive is in her sixth month. 37 For no word from God will ever fail.'
38 'I am the Lord's servant,' Mary answered. 'May your word to me be fulfilled.' Then the angel left her.

Luke 1:26–38

Christmas time can lull us into being fooled by cute cherubs on Christmas cards or familiar readings about angels, read in a monotone. Our passage is alive with emotion: hear the angel reassuring Mary, 'Do not be afraid!' (v 30). The reason for the reassurance? She was terrified!

Mary was troubled (v 29) and fearful (v 30). Looking at the angel's message we can see why: she was told that a baby would be conceived by God's power, that her child would reign for ever and that he would be the Son of God.

As Mary is presented with this astounding news, it's understandable that her first response is to ask a question: 'How will this be?' (v 34). Is there something God is asking of you that you feel you're unable to do?

. . . .

. . . .

. . . .

. . . .

. . . .

. . . .

. . . .

Day 2

The angel's answer was, 'Nothing is impossible with God' (v 37). How would Mary respond? Submitting herself to God's plan would have huge costs for her.

What step of faith could you take today based on God's Word? As you consider the cost to you, why not meditate on verse 38?

**'I am the Lord's servant …
May your word to me be fulfilled.'**

You could also listen to Handel's Messiah, 'Wonderful Counsellor' (you're bound to be able to find it online), praising the One to whom you're responding in faith.

⁴⁶ And Mary said:

'My soul glorifies the Lord
⁴⁷   and my spirit rejoices in God my Saviour,
⁴⁸ for he has been mindful
   of the humble state of his servant.
From now on all generations will call me blessed,
⁴⁹   for the Mighty One has done great things for me –
   holy is his name.
⁵⁰ His mercy extends to those who fear him,
   from generation to generation.
⁵¹ He has performed mighty deeds with his arm;
   he has scattered those who are proud in their inmost thoughts.
⁵² He has brought down rulers from their thrones
   but has lifted up the humble.
⁵³ He has filled the hungry with good things
   but has sent the rich away empty.
⁵⁴ He has helped his servant Israel,
   remembering to be merciful
⁵⁵ to Abraham and his descendants for ever,
   just as he promised our ancestors.'

Luke 1:46–55

Day 3

Mary's song, the words of which we will read today, has traditionally been called the *Magnificat* (from the Latin for 'magnifies') and has been set to music many times over the centuries. CV Stanford's 'Magnificat in G' is a beautiful piece of classical music and Chris Tomlin's 'My Soul Magnifies the Lord' is a great modern version. If you have time, why not listen to them?

Mary recognises that God has rescued her (v 47) and that he is using her despite her not being 'great' in the world's eyes (v 48). She also looks beyond herself, seeing that God will do amazing things through Jesus her son (vs 50–55).

Why not write your own song of thanks to God for all that he has done for you?

Spend time offering thanks to God and then turn your gaze upon Jesus.

When we read scripture it can be easy to forget what has gone before. Here, do we read the praise and forget that Mary had a journey of struggle and faith to get there?

Reflect on your own struggles and spiritual journey. Praise the One who saves and lifts you up (v 52), the One who works in you and through you, even in difficult times.

. . . .

. . . .

. . . .

. . . .

. . . .

. . . .

. . . .

. . . .

Day 4

[41] Every year Jesus' parents went to Jerusalem for the Festival of the Passover. [42] When he was twelve years old, they went up to the festival, according to the custom.

[43] After the festival was over, while his parents were returning home, the boy Jesus stayed behind in Jerusalem, but they were unaware of it. [44] Thinking he was in their company, they travelled on for a day. Then they began looking for him among their relatives and friends. [45] When they did not find him, they went back to Jerusalem to look for him. [46] After three days they found him in the temple courts, sitting among the teachers, listening to them and asking them questions.

[47] Everyone who heard him was amazed at his understanding and his answers. [48] When his parents saw him, they were astonished. His mother said to him, 'Son, why have you treated us like this? Your father and I have been anxiously searching for you.'

[49] 'Why were you searching for me?' he asked. 'Didn't you know I had to be in my Father's house?' [50] But they did not understand what he was saying to them.

[51] Then he went down to Nazareth with them and was obedient to them. But his mother treasured all these things in her heart. [52] And Jesus grew in wisdom and stature, and in favour with God and man.

Luke 2:41–52

Learning is not an easy process. In our reading today we see Mary and Joseph learning more about Jesus and it wasn't an easy journey.

Tucked away, just before we leave Luke's account of Jesus' childhood, is the observation that Mary treasured all these things in her heart. She has done this before (v 19). She is building up memories about Jesus from which she will one day understand not only who he is but also why he has come. This process will not be easy though.

Mary and Joseph were anxious because they didn't understand Jesus' behaviour. When have you struggled to understand what Christ is doing in your life?

. . . .

. . . .

. . . .

. . . .

. . . .

. . . .

. . . .

. . . .

. . . .

Day 4

What do you want to tell God that you have come to treasure about him?
Ask for trust when you don't understand him.

¹ In the fifteenth year of the reign of Tiberius Caesar
– when Pontius Pilate was governor of Judea, Herod
tetrarch of Galilee, his brother Philip tetrarch of Iturea
and Traconitis, and Lysanias tetrarch of Abilene –
² during the high-priesthood of Annas and Caiaphas,
the word of God came to John son of Zechariah in
the wilderness. ³ He went into all the country around
the Jordan, preaching a baptism of repentance for the
forgiveness of sins. ⁴ As it is written in the book of the
words of Isaiah the prophet:
'A voice of one calling in the wilderness,
"Prepare the way for the Lord,
    make straight paths for him. .
⁵ Every valley shall be filled in,
    every mountain and hill made low.
The crooked roads shall become straight,
    the rough ways smooth.
⁶ And all people will see God's salvation."'

Luke 3:1–6

Day 5

For a broken nation occupied by a powerful pagan empire (v 1), which had endured 400 years of prophetic silence because of their unfaithfulness, John offered the hope that God was not done with his covenant people.

How does our understanding of Isaiah's words (quoted in vs 4–6) differ from the crowd's, with their expectations of a Messiah who would renew their nationhood?

John calls the crowd to repent (v 3) but also encourages them (vs 4–6). How should we balance the call to turn from sin with the message of hope when we share our faith with others?

. . . .

. . . .

. . . .

. . . .

. . . .

. . . .

. . . .

. . . .

. . . .

. . . .

What are the problems that you see in the world or in your own life that make you long for Jesus to make 'the rough ways smooth' (v 5)?

Lift them up to him, praying for his redeeming power to be at work.

Repentance is an internal change of heart demonstrated by external changes in our behaviour. Give some time to spiritual self-examination now.

What might you need to lay down to become more fruitful for God?

Day 6

¹⁵ The people were waiting expectantly and were all wondering in their hearts if John might possibly be the Messiah. ¹⁶ John answered them all, 'I baptise you with water. But one who is more powerful than I will come, the straps of whose sandals I am not worthy to untie. He will baptise you with the Holy Spirit and fire. ¹⁷ His winnowing fork is in his hand to clear his threshing-floor and to gather the wheat into his barn, but he will burn up the chaff with unquenchable fire.' ¹⁸ And with many other words John exhorted the people and proclaimed the good news to them. ...

²¹ When all the people were being baptised, Jesus was baptised too. And as he was praying, heaven was opened ²² and the Holy Spirit descended on him in bodily form like a dove. And a voice came from heaven: 'You are my Son, whom I love; with you I am well pleased.' ²³ Now Jesus himself was about thirty years old when he began his ministry.

Luke 3:15–18,21–23a

Baptism was a sign of repentance, so what function did it serve for the only sinless human being? If you have been baptised, think about how it prepared you to serve God.

....

....

....

....

....

....

....

....

....

....

John's baptism of repentance reminds me of eating a picnic on a sandy beach on a windy day. The food starts fresh but once unpacked it becomes impossible to keep sand-free! We can repent but sin will return – we can't change our sinful natures. Only Jesus' death buries our sin, breaking its power, and raises us to new life in his resurrection, as we become one in spirit with God (Romans 6:2–7). That's what baptism needs to proclaim to the world!

Day 6

Meditate on the amazing truth that if you have been united to Christ in faith, then the Father says to you:

'You are my child, whom I love; with you I am well pleased.'

Give thanks that in Christ you're adopted into full 'sonship' in God's family. Pray through what this means for your human family.

¹ Jesus, full of the Holy Spirit, left the Jordan and was led by the Spirit into the wilderness, ² where for forty days he was tempted by the devil. He ate nothing during those days, and at the end of them he was hungry.

³ The devil said to him, 'If you are the Son of God, tell this stone to become bread.'

⁴ Jesus answered, 'It is written: "Man shall not live on bread alone."'

⁵ The devil led him up to a high place and showed him in an instant all the kingdoms of the world. ⁶ And he said to him, 'I will give you all their authority and splendour; it has been given to me, and I can give it to anyone I want to. ⁷ If you worship me, it will all be yours.'

⁸ Jesus answered, 'It is written: "Worship the Lord your God and serve him only."'

⁹ The devil led him to Jerusalem and had him stand on the highest point of the temple. 'If you are the Son of God,' he said, 'throw yourself down from here. ¹⁰ For it is written:

'"He will command his angels concerning you
    to guard you carefully;
¹¹ they will lift you up in their hands,
    so that you will not strike your foot against a stone."'

¹² Jesus answered, 'It is said: "Do not put the Lord your God to the test."'

¹³ When the devil had finished all this tempting, he left him until an opportune time.

Luke 4:1–13

Day 7

If being 'full of the Holy Spirit' (v 1) isn't enough
to defend us against temptation, what is? Our
lives must be undergirded with disciplined spiritual
practice if we're to resist Satan and be fruitful.

Thank Jesus that he did for us what was impossible
for us to do by ourselves, resisting every
temptation and living a life of perfect faith and
obedience. Praise him that he is 'our righteousness,
holiness and redemption' (1 Corinthians 2:30).

. . . .

. . . .

. . . .

. . . .

. . . .

. . . .

. . . .

. . . .

. . . .

. . . .

. . . .

. . . .

Fasting increases dependence on God, but only if we direct our hunger heavenward. Satan hates God-prioritising sacrifice and encourages us to make God's good gifts more important than their Giver (v 3). Consider whether settling for short-term gratification is hampering your spiritual growth.

God's Word (Ephesians 6:17) cuts down the lies of the enemy, which are designed to make us forget who we are in God (vs 6,7), but as with any weapon we have to learn how to wield it. We must 'let Scripture read us' through meditation, prayer, questioning and application, learning to submit ourselves fully to God.

'Thank you, Jesus, that you empathise with my weaknesses, as one who was tempted in every way but did not sin. Help me to stand firm in your strength.'

¹⁴ Jesus returned to Galilee in the power of the Spirit, and news about him spread through the whole countryside. ¹⁵ He was teaching in their synagogues, and everyone praised him.

¹⁶ He went to Nazareth, where he had been brought up, and on the Sabbath day he went into the synagogue, as was his custom. He stood up to read, ¹⁷ and the scroll of the prophet Isaiah was handed to him. Unrolling it, he found the place where it is written:

¹⁸ "The Spirit of the Lord is on me,
because he has anointed me
to proclaim good news to the poor.
He has sent me to proclaim freedom for the prisoners
and recovery of sight for the blind,
to set the oppressed free,
¹⁹ to proclaim the year of the Lord's favour."

²⁰ Then he rolled up the scroll, gave it back to the attendant and sat down. The eyes of everyone in the synagogue were fastened on him. ²¹ He began by saying to them, "Today this scripture is fulfilled in your hearing."

Luke 4:14–21

Once, as a new Christian, when dining at the home of secular Jewish friends of my wife, I insisted on saying grace before the meal. Perhaps I thought I was 'breaking the ice' so the gospel could burst forth into our conversation. Yet we ate in near silence!

Ask God for wisdom in how you represent your faith to others.

Public effectiveness for God is a measure of private devotion to God (vs 14,15). How are spiritual disciplines helping you to serve the gospel in God's strength, not your own?

Day 8

Gospel proclamation (vs 18, 19) can make us think of people wearing placards declaring 'Turn or burn', whom everyone crosses the road to avoid! But the gospel is the most powerful thing we possess (Romans 1:16) and 'We are created to infect and infiltrate culture, restoring and reclaiming what is God's' (Jefferson Bethke).

How can you live out your anointing to share the gospel so that people experience God's love, justice and life-giving hope, even before you've mentioned Jesus?

. . . .

. . . .

. . . .

. . . .

. . . .

. . . .

. . . .

. . . .

. . . .

. . . .

. . . .

Who are the spiritually poor, imprisoned, blind or oppressed in your life? Do they need practical help first or just to talk?

Pray they'll be open to you and you to them.

²² All spoke well of him and were amazed at the gracious words that came from his lips. "Isn't this Joseph's son?" they asked.

²³ Jesus said to them, "Surely you will quote this proverb to me: 'Physician, heal yourself!' And you will tell me, 'Do here in your hometown what we have heard that you did in Capernaum.'"

²⁴ "Truly I tell you," he continued, "no prophet is accepted in his hometown. ²⁵ I assure you that there were many widows in Israel in Elijah's time, when the sky was shut for three and a half years and there was a severe famine throughout the land. ²⁶ Yet Elijah was not sent to any of them, but to a widow in Zarephath in the region of Sidon. ²⁷ And there were many in Israel with leprosy in the time of Elisha the prophet, yet not one of them was cleansed – only Naaman the Syrian."

²⁸ All the people in the synagogue were furious when they heard this. ²⁹ They got up, drove him out of the town, and took him to the brow of the hill on which the town was built, in order to throw him off the cliff. ³⁰ But he walked right through the crowd and went on his way.

Luke 4:22–30

Day 9

Miracles as signposts for the open-hearted to find Jesus were wasted in Nazareth (Mark 6:5,6), for the Nazarenes wanted blessing (v 23) without acknowledging the lordship of God's anointed (v 18). We may know Jesus as Saviour, but do we rush after supernatural pyrotechnics, demanding that our needs are met, rather than responding humbly to the God-man's invitation to intimacy?

Jesus' greatest miracle is that by surrendering to him in faith we receive his righteousness in exchange for our sin (Romans 5:1,2). Truly, his love is all we need!

God is turned towards all who will turn to him, whoever they are (vs 24–27). The Nazarenes thought they had God stitched up, and the boy next door couldn't be the Messiah! Similarly, people today often dismiss Christ on the basis of preconceived ideas – and the unloving behaviour of Christians.

How are you helping people to meet the real Jesus?

'God is the kind of God who will be pleased with the one thing I have to offer – my thirst' (John Piper). Seek Jesus like someone who knows that nothing else satisfies.

Day 10

¹ One day as Jesus was standing by the Lake of Gennesaret, the people were crowding around him and listening to the word of God. ² He saw at the water's edge two boats, left there by the fishermen, who were washing their nets. ³ He got into one of the boats, the one belonging to Simon, and asked him to put out a little from shore. Then he sat down and taught the people from the boat.

⁴ When he had finished speaking, he said to Simon, "Put out into deep water, and let down the nets for a catch."

⁵ Simon answered, "Master, we've worked hard all night and haven't caught anything. But because you say so, I will let down the nets."

⁶ When they had done so, they caught such a large number of fish that their nets began to break. ⁷ So they signalled their partners in the other boat to come and help them, and they came and filled both boats so full that they began to sink.

⁸ When Simon Peter saw this, he fell at Jesus' knees and said, "Go away from me, Lord; I am a sinful man!" ⁹ For he and all his companions were astonished at the catch of fish they had taken, ¹⁰ and so were James and John, the sons of Zebedee, Simon's partners.

Then Jesus said to Simon, "Don't be afraid; from now on you will fish for people." ¹¹ So they pulled their boats up on shore, left everything and followed him.

Luke 5:1–11

Simon knew his fishing but he chose to obey Jesus anyway (v 5), and it transformed his life (vs 10,11). Our knowledge can sometimes limit our expectations, causing us to forget that we have a God of the impossible. Think of an occasion when God led you in the right direction despite it not making sense at the time. How did God build your faith through it?

. . . .

. . . .

. . . .

. . . .

. . . .

. . . .

. . . .

. . . .

Rough fishermen don't seem suitable companions for a king, so let's be encouraged that Jesus called them with all their imperfections. Why are being humble and teachable the most valuable qualities of a Jesus-follower?

Day 10

It can be hard to shake off the sense of how unworthy we are to serve Jesus (v 8).
If we aren't careful this leads us into passivity and fear, when really our dependence is
what he needs. Jesus hasn't called us because we're exceptional; he's called us to make
us exceptional in his service.

List your fears and insecurities:

List the things you take pride in:

Leave both your fear and your pride with Jesus. Ask him to turn your eyes away from
yourself and towards him. What 'nets' in your life need to be surrendered so God can
fill them for his glory?

¹¹ Soon afterward, Jesus went to a town called Nain, and his disciples and a large crowd went along with him. ¹² As he approached the town gate, a dead person was being carried out—the only son of his mother, and she was a widow. And a large crowd from the town was with her. ¹³ When the Lord saw her, his heart went out to her and he said, "Don't cry."
¹⁴ Then he went up and touched the bier they were carrying him on, and the bearers stood still. He said, "Young man, I say to you, get up!" ¹⁵ The dead man sat up and began to talk, and Jesus gave him back to his mother.
¹⁶ They were all filled with awe and praised God. "A great prophet has appeared among us," they said. "God has come to help his people." ¹⁷ This news about Jesus spread throughout Judea and the surrounding country.

Luke 7:11–17

Day 11

Luke does not mention whether the widow, lost in grief as she walks with her only son to his grave, even knows who Jesus is. There is no mention of her having any faith or hope. As far as she is concerned the situation is hopeless. She is alone, vulnerable and desolate. This is a story of Jesus taking the initiative and coming into her world, moved by compassion, to bring life.

Does it sound familiar?

Jesus turns up, touches the boy and speaks life to him. Take a moment to put yourself in the boy's shoes. Think about what it means that God's own Son turned up in our world and, by taking on death, spoke life to us.

Day 11

What difference will it make to the situations you face today to know that God is here, that he has 'come to help his people' (7:16)?

. . . .

. . . .

. . . .

. . . .

. . . .

. . . .

. . . .

. . . .

Praise God for his presence with you today.

Day 12

³⁶ When one of the Pharisees invited Jesus to have dinner with him, he went to the Pharisee's house and reclined at the table. ³⁷ A woman in that town who lived a sinful life learned that Jesus was eating at the Pharisee's house, so she came there with an alabaster jar of perfume. ³⁸ As she stood behind him at his feet weeping, she began to wet his feet with her tears. Then she wiped them with her hair, kissed them and poured perfume on them. ³⁹ When the Pharisee who had invited him saw this, he said to himself, "If this man were a prophet, he would know who is touching him and what kind of woman she is – that she is a sinner." ⁴⁰ Jesus answered him, "Simon, I have something to tell you."

"Tell me, teacher," he said.

⁴¹ "Two people owed money to a certain moneylender. One owed him five hundred denarii, and the other fifty. ⁴² Neither of them had the money to pay him back, so he forgave the debts of both. Now which of them will love him more?"

⁴³ Simon replied, "I suppose the one who had the bigger debt forgiven."

"You have judged correctly," Jesus said.

⁴⁴ Then he turned toward the woman and said to Simon, "Do you see this woman? I came into your house. You did not give me any water for my feet, but she wet my feet with her tears and wiped them with her hair. ⁴⁵ You did not give me a kiss, but this woman, from the time I entered, has not stopped kissing my feet. ⁴⁶ You did not put oil on my head, but she has poured perfume on my feet. ⁴⁷ Therefore, I tell you, her many sins have been forgiven – as her great love has shown. But whoever has been forgiven little loves little."

⁴⁸ Then Jesus said to her, "Your sins are forgiven."

⁴⁹ The other guests began to say among themselves, "Who is this who even forgives sins?"

⁵⁰ Jesus said to the woman, "Your faith has saved you; go in peace."

Luke 7:36–50

This passage is a vivid example of how our understanding of who Jesus is changes everything. This Pharisee feels he can rely on his status, his good life, his knowledge. He does not need Jesus and we see that his hospitality is pretty minimal (vs 44–46). In contrast, here is a woman relying on nothing but Jesus' forgiveness, holding nothing back, and therefore able to receive what she needs most.

'Whoever has been forgiven little loves little' (v 47). How did you come to Christ?

Write or draw the story below. If your conversion was dramatic, thank God for all he has done for you. If it has been a slow, growing process, thank God that, even though 'all have sinned and fall short of the glory of God' (Romans 3:23), you are justified freely by his grace.

Day 12

What does this passage show us about Jesus? Think, for example, of his patience with Simon (vs 40–43), his gentleness towards the woman (vs 48,50), his power (vs 48,49).

. . . .

. . . .

. . . .

. . . .

. . . .

. . . .

. . . .

. . . .

Is there something you can do today to show Jesus your love for him?

¹ After this, Jesus travelled about from one town and village to another, proclaiming the good news of the kingdom of God. The Twelve were with him, ² and also some women who had been cured of evil spirits and diseases: Mary (called Magdalene) from whom seven demons had come out; ³ Joanna the wife of Chuza, the manager of Herod's household; Susanna; and many others. These women were helping to support them out of their own means. ⁴ While a large crowd was gathering and people were coming to Jesus from town after town, he told this parable: ⁵ 'A farmer went out to sow his seed. As he was scattering the seed, some fell along the path; it was trampled on, and the birds ate it up. ⁶ Some fell on rocky ground, and when it came up, the plants withered because they had no moisture. ⁷ Other seed fell among thorns, which grew up with it and choked the plants. ⁸ Still other seed fell on good soil. It came up and yielded a crop, a hundred times more than was sown.' When he said this, he called out, 'Whoever has ears to hear, let them hear.'

⁹ His disciples asked him what this parable meant. ¹⁰ He said, 'The knowledge of the secrets of the kingdom of God has been given to you, but to others I speak in parables, so that,

> "though seeing, they may not see;
> though hearing, they may not understand."

¹¹ 'This is the meaning of the parable: the seed is the word of God. ¹² Those along the path are the ones who hear, and then the devil comes and takes away the word from their hearts, so that they may not believe and be saved. ¹³ Those on the rocky ground are the ones who receive the word with joy when they hear it, but they have no root. They believe for a while, but in the time of testing they fall away. ¹⁴ The seed that fell among thorns stands for those who hear, but as they go on their way they are choked by life's worries, riches and pleasures, and they do not mature. ¹⁵ But the seed on good soil stands for those with a noble and good heart, who hear the word, retain it, and by persevering produce a crop.'

Luke 8:1–15

Day 13

In this story we come across yet another group of people for whom faith in Jesus has changed everything. Jesus' kingdom is coming, and those who bring it once again defy the expectations of the age. Look at verses 2 and 3. These women have left their homes, their lives, their families to go with Jesus as he travels about, meeting his needs by their own hard work. Socially, this was shocking. Pharisees would certainly have frowned upon it. But to Jesus, this is what it looks like when the seed falls on good soil (v 15). Half-hearted is not an option.

. . . .

. . . .

. . . .

. . . .

. . . .

. . . .

. . . .

. . . .

Jesus' challenge in verse 8 explains why he quotes Isaiah 6:9 in verse 10. He does not wish anyone to miss the message (see 2 Peter 3:9), but he has already seen cases where resistance to his message has left people blind to the truth.

Why do you think telling parables might help with this?

Is it sometimes easier to stomach a truth if it is illustrated in a different context?

Sit in God's presence for a moment.
Ask him where he sees you in this parable.
Ask him to produce mature growth in your life.
Can you help with producing a crop?

Day 14

¹ When Jesus had called the Twelve together, he gave
them power and authority to drive out all demons and
to cure diseases, ² and he sent them out to proclaim the
kingdom of God and to heal those who were ill. ³ He told
them: 'Take nothing for the journey – no staff, no bag, no
bread, no money, no extra shirt. ⁴ Whatever house you
enter, stay there until you leave that town. ⁵ If people do
not welcome you, leave their town and shake the dust
off your feet as a testimony against them.' ⁶ So they set
out and went from village to village, proclaiming the good
news and healing people everywhere.

⁷ Now Herod the tetrarch heard about all that was going
on. And he was perplexed because some were saying that
John had been raised from the dead, ⁸ others that Elijah
had appeared, and still others that one of the prophets
of long ago had come back to life. ⁹ But Herod said, 'I
beheaded John. Who, then, is this I hear such things
about?' And he tried to see him.

Luke 9:1–9

If the readings so far have been like a jigsaw, building a picture of who Jesus is, this passage is probably a corner piece. Here we see Jesus looking ahead and giving the twelve a practice run, equipping them for days ahead when he will no longer be walking with them in person.

Jesus gives the apostles a daunting task (v 2) but he gives them the power and authority they need to carry it out (v 1). If you have time, compare this with Philippians 2:12 and 13 (working out our salvation), while God himself works in us to make that possible. Can you see links to the way God requires us to be perfect, but then provides Jesus to be our perfection for us? It's amazing!

Day 14

Look at verses 7–9. Preaching the kingdom of God in the land of Herod was risky and hard (v 3).

How does God ask you to live by kingdom rules rather than cultural rules in your life today? If God is asking something big from you, he will equip you to do it. Trust him!

Ask Jesus how you can be part of bringing his kingdom today.

[51] As the time approached for him to be taken up to heaven,
Jesus resolutely set out for Jerusalem. [52] And he sent
messengers on ahead, who went into a Samaritan village
to get things ready for him; [53] but the people there did not
welcome him, because he was heading for Jerusalem. [54] When
the disciples James and John saw this, they asked, 'Lord, do
you want us to call fire down from heaven to destroy them?'
[55] But Jesus turned and rebuked them. [56] Then he and his
disciples went to another village.

[57] As they were walking along the road, a man said to him,
'I will follow you wherever you go.'

[58] Jesus replied, 'Foxes have dens and birds have nests, but the
Son of Man has nowhere to lay his head.'

[59] He said to another man, 'Follow me.'

But he replied, 'Lord, first let me go and bury my father.'

[60] Jesus said to him, 'Let the dead bury their own dead, but
you go and proclaim the kingdom of God.'

[61] Still another said, 'I will follow you, Lord; but first let me go
back and say goodbye to my family.'

[62] Jesus replied, 'No one who puts a hand to the plough and
looks back is fit for service in the kingdom of God.'

Luke 9:51–62

Day 15

Jesus became 'obedient to death – even death on a cross' (Philippians 2:8).

Hold a picture of Jesus on the cross in your mind and quietly repeat,
'Lord, you did it for me'.

It's nice to keep your options open but sometimes you have to close them right down and choose one path. Jesus knew it was now time to head for Jerusalem and the climax of his ministry (v 51). It would have been pleasant to keep touring Galilee and enjoying the favour of the crowds, rather than entering hostile Samaritan territory (vs 52,53) and ultimately facing arrest and execution in Jerusalem. But doing the Father's will is rarely the easy option.

Can you think of a time when trusting God has meant intentionally choosing a difficult path for you? How did you cope?

What is the hardest thing about following Jesus for you just now? How are you coping with this challenge? Write down some of the challenges you are facing at the moment.

. . . .

. . . .

. . . .

. . . .

. . . .

. . . .

. . . .

. . . .

. . . .

. . . .

Remember that everyone God calls he also equips. Now invite the Holy Spirit to give you courage and strength to set your sights on following Jesus above all else.

Day 16

²⁵ On one occasion an expert in the law stood up to test Jesus. 'Teacher,' he asked, 'what must I do to inherit eternal life?'
²⁶ 'What is written in the Law?' he replied. 'How do you read it?'
²⁷ He answered, '"Love the Lord your God with all your heart and with all your soul and with all your strength and with all your mind"; and, "Love your neighbour as yourself."'
²⁸ 'You have answered correctly,' Jesus replied. 'Do this and you will live.'
²⁹ But he wanted to justify himself, so he asked Jesus, 'And who is my neighbour?'
³⁰ In reply Jesus said: 'A man was going down from Jerusalem to Jericho, when he was attacked by robbers. They stripped him of his clothes, beat him and went away, leaving him half-dead. ³¹ A priest happened to be going down the same road, and when he saw the man, he passed by on the other side. ³² So too, a Levite, when he came to the place and saw him, passed by on the other side. ³³ But a Samaritan, as he travelled, came where the man was; and when he saw him, he took pity on him. ³⁴ He went to him and bandaged his wounds, pouring on oil and wine. Then he put the man on his own donkey, brought him to an inn and took care of him. ³⁵ The next day he took out two denarii and gave them to the innkeeper. "Look after him," he said, "and when I return, I will reimburse you for any extra expense you may have."
³⁶ 'Which of these three do you think was a neighbour to the man who fell into the hands of robbers?'
³⁷ The expert in the law replied, 'The one who had mercy on him.' Jesus told him, 'Go and do likewise.'

Luke 10:25–37

What is the minimum I can do to prove my love for God? Perhaps this is the thought behind the question in verse 29. In other words, 'What can I get away with?' But this is always the wrong question. When you are seized by the utterly generous, undeserved and unremitting love of God, the natural response is to ask, 'How can I give him the maximum?'

. . . .

. . . .

. . . .

. . . .

. . . .

. . . .

. . . .

Meditate on Jesus' summary of the Law, lingering over what each word adds to our picture of God's own character and nature.

> **'"Love the Lord your God**
> **with all your heart**
> **and with all your soul**
> **and with all your strength**
> **and with all your mind";**
> **and, "Love your neighbour as yourself."'**

Day 16

'Everyone needs compassion ... the kindness of a Saviour' (Ben Fielding and Reuben Morgan, © Hillsong Publishing, 2006). Think of the evidence of God's kindness to you and let it encourage you to worship him with all your heart.

How does the worship you express with words and music overflow into compassion in your daily life? Let the Holy Spirit show you where you need to get off your donkey and apply oil and wine to a wounded person.

³⁸ As Jesus and his disciples were on their way, he came
to a village where a woman named Martha opened her
home to him. ³⁹ She had a sister called Mary, who sat at
the Lord's feet listening to what he said. ⁴⁰ But Martha
was distracted by all the preparations that had to be
made. She came to him and asked, 'Lord, don't you care
that my sister has left me to do the work by myself? Tell
her to help me!'
⁴¹ 'Martha, Martha,' the Lord answered, 'you are worried
and upset about many things, ⁴² but few things are needed
– or indeed only one. Mary has chosen what is better,
and it will not be taken away from her.'

Luke 10:38–42

Day 17

Martha was a hospitable lady (v 38), but whereas her sister, Mary, knew how to slow down (v 39), Martha seemed to have been more driven (v 40). With what we know about Jesus, it's hard for us to imagine how you could be distracted by anything else when he had come to stay. But perhaps we also get distracted from the things Jesus is saying to us because we are too busy doing good things.

Are you more naturally inclined to active service or to quiet contemplation?

. . . .

. . . .

. . . .

. . . .

. . . .

. . . .

. . . .

. . . .

. . . .

. . . .

. . . .

. . . .

. . . .

. . . .

. . . .

A healthy relationship with God involves both. Contemplation means being without doing, stopping to listen attentively, resting in God's love. Sometimes we try to validate our living by the number of things we achieve, and like Martha we can get unduly worried about them (v 41).

Ask Jesus to help you walk with him at his pace, like his first disciples (v 38), stopping along the way for rest and refreshment.

When are your Mary moments – times when you stop to be with Jesus and listen to him? How can you cherish and protect those times so the rush of life does not crowd them out?

'Be still before the LORD and wait patiently for him' (Psalm 37:7). For a few minutes, try to be as still as you can by repeating in your mind the phrase, 'Lord, you are here'. Sit comfortably, relax your body, breathe more slowly and just be in God's presence.

Day 18

¹ One day Jesus was praying in a certain place. When he finished, one of his disciples said to him, 'Lord, teach us to pray, just as John taught his disciples.'
² He said to them, 'When you pray, say:

"'Father,
hallowed be your name,
your kingdom come.
³ Give us each day our daily bread.
⁴ Forgive us our sins,
for we also forgive everyone who sins against us.
And lead us not into temptation.'"

⁵ Then Jesus said to them, 'Suppose you have a friend, and you go to him at midnight and say, "Friend, lend me three loaves of bread; ⁶ a friend of mine on a journey has come to me, and I have no food to offer him." ⁷ And suppose the one inside answers, "Don't bother me. The door is already locked, and my children and I are in bed. I can't get up and give you anything." ⁸ I tell you, even though he will not get up and give you the bread because of friendship, yet because of your shameless audacity he will surely get up and give you as much as you need.
⁹ 'So I say to you: ask and it will be given to you; seek and you will find; knock and the door will be opened to you.
¹⁰ For everyone who asks receives; the one who seeks finds; and to the one who knocks, the door will be opened.'

Luke 11:1–10

What are the habits, beliefs, attitudes and circumstances in your life
that keep you from prayer?

Jesus gently demolishes stumbling blocks that might keep us from prayer:

- *I don't know how to pray (v 1)*. Look at the simple framework for praying that Jesus
  gives (vs 2–4). We can fill in the gaps and make this prayer our prayer.

- *God is not interested in my prayers*. Prayer is based on the character of God, and he is
  a good Father who wants us to come to him with our requests (v 2).

- *Nothing happened so I gave up praying*. Often we have to persist in prayer. But if even
  a lazy friend can be stirred to action by 'shameless audacity' (v 8), how much more
  will God listen to us when we keep on praying?

Day 18

Make the Lord's Prayer your own by asking questions like, how can I 'hallow' your name, Lord? Where do I long to see God's kingdom? What is my daily bread? What are my sins? Who do I need to forgive? How am I tempted?

Father

Hallowed be your name

Your kingdom come

Give us each day our daily bread

Forgive us our sins

For we also forgive everyone who sins against us

And lead us not into temptation

¹³ Someone in the crowd said to him, 'Teacher, tell my brother to divide the inheritance with me.'

¹⁴ Jesus replied, 'Man, who appointed me a judge or an arbiter between you?' ¹⁵ Then he said to them, 'Watch out! Be on your guard against all kinds of greed; life does not consist in an abundance of possessions.'

¹⁶ And he told them this parable: 'The ground of a certain rich man yielded an abundant harvest. ¹⁷ He thought to himself, "What shall I do? I have no place to store my crops."

¹⁸ 'Then he said, "This is what I'll do. I will tear down my barns and build bigger ones, and there I will store my surplus grain. ¹⁹ And I'll say to myself, 'You have plenty of grain laid up for many years. Take life easy; eat, drink and be merry.'"

²⁰ 'But God said to him, "You fool! This very night your life will be demanded from you. Then who will get what you have prepared for yourself?"

²¹ 'This is how it will be with whoever stores up things for themselves but is not rich towards God.'

Luke 12:13–21

Day 19

In a 'consumer culture', we don't view our lives as the sum of what we can offer to others – family, community and society – but what we can take from life. We build our identity around accumulation and consumption, whether of income, possessions, experiences, entertainment or relationships.

Jesus warns us to 'Be on your guard against all kinds of greed.'

What different types of greed can you think of?

What kinds of thing are you most tempted to be greedy for?

Have you bought into the myth of consumerism? Take some time to be quiet and allow God to search your heart. Has accumulating stuff – wealth, possessions, experiences – become the thing that gives you security?

Meditate on what it means to be 'rich towards God'.

How do our riches in Christ give us greater security than anything the world has to offer us? How can you prepare your heart to face death without fear?

Spend time thanking God for your eternal inheritance in Christ.

¹ Now there were some present at that time who told Jesus about the Galileans whose blood Pilate had mixed with their sacrifices. ² Jesus answered, 'Do you think that these Galileans were worse sinners than all the other Galileans because they suffered this way? ³ I tell you, no! But unless you repent, you too will all perish. ⁴ Or those eighteen who died when the tower in Siloam fell on them – do you think they were more guilty than all the others living in Jerusalem? ⁵ I tell you, no! But unless you repent, you too will all perish.'

⁶ Then he told this parable: 'A man had a fig-tree growing in his vineyard, and he went to look for fruit on it but did not find any. ⁷ So he said to the man who took care of the vineyard, "For three years now I've been coming to look for fruit on this fig-tree and haven't found any. Cut it down! Why should it use up the soil?"

⁸ "'Sir," the man replied, "leave it alone for one more year, and I'll dig round it and fertilise it. ⁹ If it bears fruit next year, fine! If not, then cut it down.'"

Luke 13:1–9

Why do disasters happen? As we see events in the world, it is often a question that troubles us and can shake our faith. Reflecting on both a recent natural disaster and an act of state-sponsored terrorism, Jesus makes it clear (vs 2–5) that these were not specific acts of divine judgement against those involved. Yet all of us face a similar fate, no matter how our lives end, unless we place ourselves in God's care through repentance and faith.

Wait on the Lord in silence for a minute or two. If your thoughts wander, gently return your focus to him.

. . . .

. . . .

. . . .

. . . .

. . . .

. . . .

. . . .

. . . .

. . . .

. . . .

. . . .

. . . .

Day 20

Meditate on Jesus' parable of a gardener and the fig-tree (vs 6–9).
What do you discover about God's patience?

> **'[God] is patient with you, not wanting anyone to perish,
> but everyone to come to repentance' (2 Peter 3:9).**

Thank God for his patience that allowed you to come to repentance.
Pray for those you know who don't know the Lord; that his patience
would give them time to turn to him.

¹⁰ On a Sabbath Jesus was teaching in one of the synagogues, ¹¹ and a woman was there who had been crippled by a spirit for eighteen years. She was bent over and could not straighten up at all. ¹² When Jesus saw her, he called her forward and said to her, 'Woman, you are set free from your infirmity.' ¹³ Then he put his hands on her, and immediately she straightened up and praised God. ¹⁴ Indignant because Jesus had healed on the Sabbath, the synagogue leader said to the people, 'There are six days for work. So come and be healed on those days, not on the Sabbath.'

¹⁵ The Lord answered him, 'You hypocrites! Doesn't each of you on the Sabbath untie your ox or donkey from the stall and lead it out to give it water? ¹⁶ Then should not this woman, a daughter of Abraham, whom Satan has kept bound for eighteen long years, be set free on the Sabbath day from what bound her?'

¹⁷ When he said this, all his opponents were humiliated, but the people were delighted with all the wonderful things he was doing.

Luke 13:10–17

Day 21

From a religious perspective, this woman did not have a lot going for her. First, she was a woman, and considered by the culture of the time to be less than a man. Many would assume she was crippled as a punishment for some sin in her or her family's life. She was considered to be demonically oppressed (v 11).

But Jesus didn't ignore her. She probably inhabited the fringes of the synagogue, but he called her into the centre (v 12). He spoke to her and even put his hands on her (v 13). He reminded the synagogue leader that the woman was 'a daughter of Abraham' (v 16) and not just the sum of her problems. The religious leaders had lost sight of the true purpose of the law, which was love and compassion.

Have you allowed religious judgement to colour your view of those around you? If so, take some time to ask God to pour his grace on them – and also on you.

Think about how Jesus shows love to the poor, sick and marginalised. Take time to delight in all the wonderful things Jesus has done, like the people did (v 17).

. . . .

. . . .

. . . .

. . . .

. . . .

. . . .

. . . .

. . . .

. . . .

. . . .

¹ One Sabbath, when Jesus went to eat in the house of a prominent Pharisee, he was being carefully watched.
² There in front of him was a man suffering from abnormal swelling of his body. ³ Jesus asked the Pharisees and experts in the law, 'Is it lawful to heal on the Sabbath or not?' ⁴ But they remained silent. So taking hold of the man, he healed him and sent him on his way.
⁵ Then he asked them, 'If one of you has a child or an ox that falls into a well on the Sabbath day, will you not immediately pull it out?' ⁶ And they had nothing to say.
⁷ When he noticed how the guests picked the places of honour at the table, he told them this parable: ⁸ 'When someone invites you to a wedding feast, do not take the place of honour, for a person more distinguished than you may have been invited. ⁹ If so, the host who invited both of you will come and say to you, "Give this person your seat." Then, humiliated, you will have to take the least important place. ¹⁰ But when you are invited, take the lowest place, so that when your host comes, he will say to you, "Friend, move up to a better place." Then you will be honoured in the presence of all the other guests. ¹¹ For all those who exalt themselves will be humbled, and those who humble themselves will be exalted.'

Luke 14:1–11

What do you delight in at the moment? Reflect on the truth that the Lord delights in you (Psalm 147:11).

. . . .

. . . .

. . . .

. . . .

. . . .

. . . .

. . . .

. . . .

. . . .

. . . .

When I talk with people who aren't Jesus-followers, they often say, 'Well, I'm not a particularly religious person'. One of the great myths of our culture is that Jesus came to make us more religious. But Jesus didn't come to make us more religious, but to show us grace.

Day 22

Jesus deals with the great myth of religion: that we are accepted by our efforts, rather than God's grace. Those who felt entitled took the best places at the table (vs 7,8), but risked discovering they were not as worthy as they thought (v 9). The right response to grace is humility (v 10). From there, God can invite us up to eat at the best place (v 10).

Was Jesus really breaking the Sabbath in healing the woman? Think about ways in which you might prioritise following rules and social conventions over true obedience to God.

Have you been trying to please God through your own efforts?

Take some time to thank him that when we come to him with empty hands he says 'Friend, move up to a better place.'

¹² Then Jesus said to his host, 'When you give a luncheon or dinner, do not invite your friends, your brothers or sisters, your relatives, or your rich neighbours; if you do, they may invite you back and so you will be repaid. ¹³ But when you give a banquet, invite the poor, the crippled, the lame, the blind, ¹⁴ and you will be blessed. Although they cannot repay you, you will be repaid at the resurrection of the righteous.'

¹⁵ When one of those at the table with him heard this, he said to Jesus, 'Blessed is the one who will eat at the feast in the kingdom of God.'

¹⁶ Jesus replied: 'A certain man was preparing a great banquet and invited many guests. ¹⁷ At the time of the banquet he sent his servant to tell those who had been invited, "Come, for everything is now ready."

¹⁸ 'But they all alike began to make excuses. The first said, "I have just bought a field, and I must go and see it. Please excuse me."

¹⁹ 'Another said, "I have just bought five yoke of oxen, and I'm on my way to try them out. Please excuse me."

²⁰ 'Still another said, "I have just got married, so I can't come."

²¹ 'The servant came back and reported this to his master. Then the owner of the house became angry and ordered his servant, "Go out quickly into the streets and alleys of the town and bring in the poor, the crippled, the blind and the lame."

²² '"Sir," the servant said, "what you ordered has been done, but there is still room."

²³ 'Then the master told his servant, "Go out to the roads and country lanes and compel them to come in, so that my house will be full. ²⁴ I tell you, not one of those who were invited will get a taste of my banquet."'

Luke 14:12–24

Day 23

'For I was hungry, and you fed me' (Matthew 25:35, NLT). Today, thank God for anyone who's met your physical needs in Jesus' name.

Have you ever thought that God loves parties? Jesus is the host of the banquet to which we're all invited! We rarely think of God as a host, but he is. Of those he invites, not all respond (vs 18–21). Yet, the passion of the host is undimmed; he will not rest until his house is full (v 23). He has, of course, a particular concern for the poor (v 21) and encourages us to do likewise (vs 12–14). As Jesus hosts us, he encourages us to host others, that every seat at the banquet might be taken.

. . . .

. . . .

. . . .

. . . .

. . . .

. . . .

. . . .

. . . .

. . . .

. . . .

. . . .

. . . .

Jesus invites you to his grace-banquet today. Will you receive all he has for you?
How can you share the feast with others?

Look back over the passage.
What does God want to say to you today?

²⁵ Large crowds were travelling with Jesus, and turning to them he said: ²⁶ 'If anyone comes to me and does not hate father and mother, wife and children, brothers and sisters – yes, even their own life – such a person cannot be my disciple. ²⁷ And whoever does not carry their cross and follow me cannot be my disciple.

²⁸ 'Suppose one of you wants to build a tower. Won't you first sit down and estimate the cost to see if you have enough money to complete it? ²⁹ For if you lay the foundation and are not able to finish it, everyone who sees it will ridicule you, ³⁰ saying, "This person began to build and wasn't able to finish."

³¹ 'Or suppose a king is about to go to war against another king. Won't he first sit down and consider whether he is able with ten thousand men to oppose the one coming against him with twenty thousand? ³² If he is not able, he will send a delegation while the other is still a long way off and will ask for terms of peace. ³³ In the same way, those of you who do not give up everything you have cannot be my disciples.

³⁴ 'Salt is good, but if it loses its saltiness, how can it be made salty again? ³⁵ It is fit neither for the soil nor for the manure heap; it is thrown out.

'Whoever has ears to hear, let them hear.'

Luke 14:25–35

'Christ died for sinners.' What do these words mean to you personally?

. . . .

. . . .

. . . .

. . . .

. . . .

. . . .

. . . .

. . . .

The German pastor and martyr Dietrich Bonhoeffer explains:

'The cross is laid on every Christian. The first Christ-suffering which every man must experience is the call to abandon the attachments of this world … When Christ calls a man, he bids him come and die' (*The Cost of Discipleship*).

Jesus is saying that our affection and commitment to him should be so great that no other regard or pursuit in life competes with it. This requires careful deliberation by those who are considering giving their lives to him, and by those of us who have already decided to do so! Jesus is demanding everything from us, as only he may do.

Ask the Holy Spirit to trouble your conscience about anything (or anyone) that is vying with God for your affections. What do you find hardest to give up for following Jesus?

Do you feel that following Jesus is worth giving up everything for? Why or why not?

Ask the Father to help you to see that Jesus is worth everything. Invite the Holy Spirit to deepen your delight in the Son, and to give you greater understanding of who he is and all that he has done.

¹ Now the tax collectors and sinners were all gathering round to hear Jesus. ² But the Pharisees and the teachers of the law muttered, 'This man welcomes sinners, and eats with them.'
³ Then Jesus told them this parable: ⁴ 'Suppose one of you has a hundred sheep and loses one of them. Doesn't he leave the ninety-nine in the open country and go after the lost sheep until he finds it? ⁵ And when he finds it, he joyfully puts it on his shoulders ⁶ and goes home. Then he calls his friends and neighbours together and says, "Rejoice with me; I have found my lost sheep." ⁷ I tell you that in the same way there will be more rejoicing in heaven over one sinner who repents than over ninety-nine righteous people who do not need to repent.
⁸ 'Or suppose a woman has ten silver coins and loses one. Doesn't she light a lamp, sweep the house and search carefully until she finds it? ⁹ And when she finds it, she calls her friends and neighbours together and says, "Rejoice with me; I have found my lost coin." ¹⁰ In the same way, I tell you, there is rejoicing in the presence of the angels of God over one sinner who repents.'

Luke 15:1–10

Day 25

Have you ever seen a map zoom out from street level to outer space? In your mind's eye (or online if you wish), travel from the place where you are currently up into the clouds and out into space, until the earth and sun disappear in the vastness of the universe. God knows exactly where you are and who you are. That's worth some awestruck praise!

Jesus ate with sinners. Imagine he came for dinner with you in your home. What would you talk to him about? What concerns would you share, and what questions would you ask?

. . . .

. . . .

. . . .

. . . .

. . . .

. . . .

. . . .

. . . .

. . . .

. . . .

Talk to Jesus now about these things in prayer. Listen to what he might be saying to you. If you feel inadequate or unworthy, remember that 'This man welcomes sinners, and eats with them.'

This is the mission of the man from heaven: 'to seek and to save what was lost' (19:10). Meditate on the reality of heaven: great joy when sinners repent.

As the Father sent the Son, so the Son has sent us. What will you do today to fulfil your calling to be part of God's great search and rescue team?

¹¹ Jesus continued: 'There was a man who had two sons. ¹² The younger one said to his father, "Father, give me my share of the estate." So he divided his property between them.

¹³ 'Not long after that, the younger son got together all he had, set off for a distant country and there squandered his wealth in wild living. ¹⁴ After he had spent everything, there was a severe famine in that whole country, and he began to be in need. ¹⁵ So he went and hired himself out to a citizen of that country, who sent him to his fields to feed pigs. ¹⁶ He longed to fill his stomach with the pods that the pigs were eating, but no one gave him anything.

¹⁷ 'When he came to his senses, he said, "How many of my father's hired servants have food to spare, and here I am starving to death! ¹⁸ I will set out and go back to my father and say to him: Father, I have sinned against heaven and against you. ¹⁹ I am no longer worthy to be called your son; make me like one of your hired servants." ²⁰ So he got up and went to his father.

'But while he was still a long way off, his father saw him and was filled with compassion for him; he ran to his son, threw his arms round him and kissed him. ²¹ 'The son said to him, "Father, I have sinned against heaven and against you. I am no longer worthy to be called your son."

²² 'But the father said to his servants, "Quick! Bring the best robe and put it on him. Put a ring on his finger and sandals on his feet. ²³ Bring the fattened calf and kill it. Let's have a feast and celebrate. ²⁴ For this son of mine was dead and is alive again; he was lost and is found." So they began to celebrate.

²⁵ 'Meanwhile, the elder son was in the field. When he came near the house, he heard music and dancing. ²⁶ So he called one of the servants and asked him what was going on. ²⁷ "Your brother has come," he replied, "and your father has killed the fattened calf because he has him back safe and sound."

²⁸ 'The elder brother became angry and refused to go in. So his father went out and pleaded with him. ²⁹ But he answered his father, "Look! All these years I've been slaving for you and never disobeyed your orders. Yet you never gave me even a young goat so I could celebrate with my friends. ³⁰ But when this son of yours who has squandered your property with prostitutes comes home, you kill the fattened calf for him!"

³¹ '"My son," the father said, "you are always with me, and everything I have is yours. ³² But we had to celebrate and be glad, because this brother of yours was dead and is alive again; he was lost and is found."'

Luke 15:11–32

Reread the story, putting yourself in the place of each son. What would they have thought and felt at each point? Who do you identify with most?

. . . .

. . . .

. . . .

. . . .

. . . .

. . . .

. . . .

Which of the two lifestyles is the greater temptation for you: ignoring all the rules, or trying to earn favour by keeping all the rules?

. . . .

. . . .

. . . .

. . . .

. . . .

. . . .

. . . .

Day 26

Imagine God running to you while you are a long way off, throwing his arms around you and kissing you. What do you want to say to your heavenly Father?

¹⁹ 'There was a rich man who was dressed in purple and fine linen and lived in luxury every day. ²⁰ At his gate was laid a beggar named Lazarus, covered with sores ²¹ and longing to eat what fell from the rich man's table. Even the dogs came and licked his sores.

²² 'The time came when the beggar died and the angels carried him to Abraham's side. The rich man also died and was buried. ²³ In Hades, where he was in torment, he looked up and saw Abraham far away, with Lazarus by his side. ²⁴ So he called to him, "Father Abraham, have pity on me and send Lazarus to dip the tip of his finger in water and cool my tongue, because I am in agony in this fire."

²⁵ 'But Abraham replied, "Son, remember that in your lifetime you received your good things, while Lazarus received bad things, but now he is comforted here and you are in agony. ²⁶ And besides all this, between us and you a great chasm has been set in place, so that those who want to go from here to you cannot, nor can anyone cross over from there to us."

²⁷ 'He answered, "Then I beg you, father, send Lazarus to my family, ²⁸ for I have five brothers. Let him warn them, so that they will not also come to this place of torment."

²⁹ 'Abraham replied, "They have Moses and the Prophets; let them listen to them."

³⁰ '"No, father Abraham," he said, "but if someone from the dead goes to them, they will repent."

³¹ 'He said to him, "If they do not listen to Moses and the Prophets, they will not be convinced even if someone rises from the dead."'

Luke 16:19–31

Day 27

In a culture that equated wealth with blessing, what happened in the story was shocking: the rich man went to hell whilst the beggar was carried to heaven. Jesus is not saying there is something intrinsically righteous about the poor, or worthy of damnation about the rich, but plainly stating that those who invest all their hope in this life have none left for the next (v 25).

Reflect on what you are putting your trust in.
Ask God to give you an eternal perspective.

Would evangelism be easier if God did more spectacular miracles, like raising the dead, to convince people that the gospel is true?

. . . .

. . . .

. . . .

. . . .

. . . .

. . . .

. . . .

Who in your life do you want to see come to follow Jesus?
What can you do to share the good news with them?
Pray for them now.

Spurgeon said: 'If sinners be damned, at least let them leap to hell over our bodies. If they will perish, let them perish with our arms about their knees. Let no one go there unwarned and unprayed for.'

Ask the Holy Spirit to give you boldness and wisdom in sharing the good news.

¹¹ Now on his way to Jerusalem, Jesus travelled along the border between Samaria and Galilee. ¹² As he was going into a village, ten men who had leprosy met him. They stood at a distance ¹³ and called out in a loud voice, 'Jesus, Master, have pity on us!'
¹⁴ When he saw them, he said, 'Go, show yourselves to the priests.' And as they went, they were cleansed.
¹⁵ One of them, when he saw he was healed, came back, praising God in a loud voice. ¹⁶ He threw himself at Jesus' feet and thanked him – and he was a Samaritan.
¹⁷ Jesus asked, 'Were not all ten cleansed? Where are the other nine? ¹⁸ Has no one returned to give praise to God except this foreigner?' ¹⁹ Then he said to him, 'Rise and go; your faith has made you well.'

Luke 17:11–19

We often talk about time with God as a 'quiet time'. But many people in Luke's Gospel praise God in a loud voice (see 19:37), and it's very appropriate!

Whether it's your habit or not, stir yourself to say or sing out loud your thanks to God for all he has done for you.

Those with leprosy were the outcasts of the ancient world. Contagious and ceremonially unclean, the moment their affliction was discovered they were cast out of their community (see Leviticus 13:45,46). They were spiritual outcasts too: the Jewish tradition held that those with leprosy were suffering physically for their sins (the church has sometimes made the same mistake with those who are sick).

How does the way Jesus treat the lepers revolutionise our understanding of holiness?

. . . .

. . . .

. . . .

. . . .

. . . .

. . . .

. . . .

. . . .

Day 28

Once healed, what would they do first? One of them realised that something else was more important than any of these things: he ran to Jesus (vs 15,16). Healing and forgiveness from God allows us to do many things but worshipping him in glad response is where we should always start.

Look back at some of the challenges you wrote down on day 15. Have you seen God at work in them? If so, thank him now.

The grace we have received on this day alone ought to be enough to keep us praising God for all eternity. You're alive and forgiven, and that's just the start. Don't miss a single opportunity today to thank God as he blesses you, even if it slows your day down!

¹ Then Jesus told his disciples a parable to show them
that they should always pray and not give up. ² He said:
'In a certain town there was a judge who neither feared
God nor cared what people thought. ³ And there was
a widow in that town who kept coming to him with the
plea, "Grant me justice against my adversary."

⁴ 'For some time he refused. But finally he said to himself,
"Even though I don't fear God or care what people think,
⁵ yet because this widow keeps bothering me, I will see
that she gets justice, so that she won't eventually come
and attack me!"'

⁶ And the Lord said, 'Listen to what the unjust judge says.
⁷ And will not God bring about justice for his chosen
ones, who cry out to him day and night? Will he keep
putting them off? ⁸ I tell you, he will see that they get
justice, and quickly. However, when the Son of Man
comes, will he find faith on the earth?'

Luke 18:1–8

Day 29

Meditate on the eternity of God. Watch the second hand tick on a clock and consider that 'with the Lord a day is like a thousand years, and a thousand years are like a day' (2 Peter 3:8). He's beyond time, he made it – now that's a mystery to inspire worship!

Why do you think Jesus told us a parable in order to keep us praying and not give up? Because very often we're tempted to give up praying! We all experience tiredness, frustration, even hopelessness in our prayers. This is the 'now and not yet' tension of the kingdom of God.

Are there people or situations you have given up praying for?
Write them down, and pray for them again now.

Jesus chooses an uncaring judge to contrast with our loving heavenly Father: if even this rotten judge gives an answer in response to the widow's determination then surely our wonderful God is only too willing to answer our prayers?

> **'Prayer is not overcoming God's reluctance.**
> **It is laying hold of God's willingness.'**
> (Attributed to Martin Luther)

Do you have faith that God will see that you get justice, and quickly? It can be hard to believe at times, but remind yourself of God's promises, and his invitation to hammer on the door of heaven: 'You who call on the LORD, give yourselves no rest, and give him no rest till he establishes Jerusalem and makes her the praise of the earth' (Isaiah 62:6,7).

Day 30

²⁸ After Jesus had said this, he went on ahead, going up to Jerusalem. ²⁹ As he approached Bethphage and Bethany at the hill called the Mount of Olives, he sent two of his disciples, saying to them, ³⁰ 'Go to the village ahead of you, and as you enter it, you will find a colt tied there, which no one has ever ridden. Untie it and bring it here. ³¹ If anyone asks you, "Why are you untying it?" say, "The Lord needs it."'

³² Those who were sent ahead went and found it just as he had told them. ³³ As they were untying the colt, its owners asked them, 'Why are you untying the colt?'

³⁴ They replied, 'The Lord needs it.'

³⁵ They brought it to Jesus, threw their cloaks on the colt and put Jesus on it. ³⁶ As he went along, people spread their cloaks on the road.

³⁷ When he came near the place where the road goes down the Mount of Olives, the whole crowd of disciples began joyfully to praise God in loud voices for all the miracles they had seen:

³⁸ 'Blessed is the king who comes in the name of the Lord!'

'Peace in heaven and glory in the highest!'

³⁹ Some of the Pharisees in the crowd said to Jesus, 'Teacher, rebuke your disciples!'

⁴⁰ 'I tell you,' he replied, 'if they keep quiet, the stones will cry out.'

⁴¹ As he approached Jerusalem and saw the city, he wept over it ⁴² and said, 'If you, even you, had only known on this day what would bring you peace – but now it is hidden from your eyes. ⁴³ The days will come upon you when your enemies will build an embankment against you and encircle you and hem you in on every side. ⁴⁴ They will dash you to the ground, you and the children within your walls. They will not leave one stone on another, because you did not recognise the time of God's coming to you.'

Luke 19:28–44

The white buildings that lie ahead, glinting in the morning sunlight, are part of the view of Jerusalem – the city whose name means peace. The man on the donkey, whose gentle eyes are dancing along with the surrounding children, is Jesus – at whose birth angels tore open the sky to announce peace (Luke 2:14). The crowd of pilgrims, throwing down their cloaks ahead of the procession, are singing songs of peace (v 38).

Peace. The longing of today's frenetic and divided world.

But suddenly the celebrations screech to a halt: Jesus has burst into tears. He foresees the destruction of the city in AD 70: the siege machines, the mass crucifixions, the women's screams. 'If you … had only known … what would bring you peace,' he weeps (v 42). '[But] All this will happen because you did not recognise the time when God came to save you' (v 44, NCV).

If only our world knew what would bring peace.

Are you ready to meet God today? Have you quietened your heart? Have you cleared space in your thoughts? Take the time you need to prepare, because you don't want to miss his voice if he speaks.

Day 30

Where are you longing to see peace? On the international stage? In your workplace? Your family? Your heart?

The Prince of Peace has an appointment with you today. Keep that appointment now: enjoy time with him, and ask him to fill you with his peace.

¹ Now the Festival of Unleavened Bread, called the Passover, was approaching, ² and the chief priests and the teachers of the law were looking for some way to get rid of Jesus, for they were afraid of the people. ³ Then Satan entered Judas, called Iscariot, one of the Twelve. ⁴ And Judas went to the chief priests and the officers of the temple guard and discussed with them how he might betray Jesus. ⁵ They were delighted and agreed to give him money. ⁶ He consented, and watched for an opportunity to hand Jesus over to them when no crowd was present.

⁷ Then came the day of Unleavened Bread on which the Passover lamb had to be sacrificed. ⁸ Jesus sent Peter and John, saying, 'Go and make preparations for us to eat the Passover.'

⁹ 'Where do you want us to prepare for it?' they asked.

¹⁰ He replied, 'As you enter the city, a man carrying a jar of water will meet you. Follow him to the house that he enters, ¹¹ and say to the owner of the house, "The Teacher asks: where is the guest room, where I may eat the Passover with my disciples?" ¹² He will show you a large room upstairs, all furnished. Make preparations there.'

¹³ They left and found things just as Jesus had told them. So they prepared the Passover.

¹⁴ When the hour came, Jesus and his apostles reclined at the table. ¹⁵ And he said to them, 'I have eagerly desired to eat this Passover with you before I suffer. ¹⁶ For I tell you, I will not eat it again until it finds fulfilment in the kingdom of God.'

¹⁷ After taking the cup, he gave thanks and said, 'Take this and divide it among you. ¹⁸ For I tell you I will not drink again from the fruit of the vine until the kingdom of God comes.'

¹⁹ And he took bread, gave thanks and broke it, and gave it to them, saying, 'This is my body given for you; do this in remembrance of me.'

²⁰ In the same way, after the supper he took the cup, saying, 'This cup is the new covenant in my blood, which is poured out for you.'

Luke 22:1–20

Day 31

We meet Jesus and the disciples at the Last Supper, where Jesus bridges the old and new covenants by celebrating the Passover. These preparations for the Passover would have been very normal for both Jesus and the disciples, having celebrated the festival annually all their lives. Yet, God is doing something new, different and divinely planned around the preparations this time.

Bread and wine had been heavily symbolic for the Jews since their last meal in Egypt as slaves. Here Jesus gives the emblems another layer of significance; and just as he asked his disciples to do on that fateful night, so his followers still eat bread and drink wine to recall his sacrifice (v 19).

What habits and routines can you weave into your life to remind yourself of Jesus?

Thank Jesus for the amazing gift of his body and blood, given for you.

. . . .

. . . .

. . . .

. . . .

. . . .

. . . .

. . . .

. . . .

. . . .

. . . .

. . . .

. . . .

. . . .

. . . .

. . . .

. . . .

.

'Father, we give you praise for your Son, Jesus.
We thank you that we are part of your kingdom because of him!'

Day 32

³⁹ Jesus went out as usual to the Mount of Olives, and his disciples followed him.
⁴⁰ On reaching the place, he said to them, 'Pray that you will not fall into temptation.'
⁴¹ He withdrew about a stone's throw beyond them, knelt down and prayed, ⁴² 'Father, if you are willing, take this cup from me; yet not my will, but yours be done.' ⁴³ An angel from heaven appeared to him and strengthened him. ⁴⁴ And being in anguish, he prayed more earnestly, and his sweat was like drops of blood falling to the ground.

⁴⁵ When he rose from prayer and went back to the disciples, he found them asleep, exhausted from sorrow. ⁴⁶ 'Why are you sleeping?' he asked them. 'Get up and pray so that you will not fall into temptation.'

⁴⁷ While he was still speaking a crowd came up, and the man who was called Judas, one of the Twelve, was leading them. He approached Jesus to kiss him, ⁴⁸ but Jesus asked him, 'Judas, are you betraying the Son of Man with a kiss?'

⁴⁹ When Jesus' followers saw what was going to happen, they said, 'Lord, should we strike with our swords?' ⁵⁰ And one of them struck the servant of the high priest, cutting off his right ear.

⁵¹ But Jesus answered, 'No more of this!' And he touched the man's ear and healed him.

⁵² Then Jesus said to the chief priests, the officers of the temple guard, and the elders, who had come for him, 'Am I leading a rebellion, that you have come with swords and clubs? ⁵³ Every day I was with you in the temple courts, and you did not lay a hand on me. But this is your hour – when darkness reigns.'

⁵⁴ Then seizing him, they led him away and took him into the house of the high priest. Peter followed at a distance. ⁵⁵ And when some there had kindled a fire in the middle of the courtyard and had sat down together, Peter sat down with them. ⁵⁶ A servant-girl saw him seated there in the firelight. She looked closely at him and said, 'This man was with him.'

⁵⁷ But he denied it. 'Woman, I don't know him,' he said.

⁵⁸ A little later someone else saw him and said, 'You also are one of them.'

'Man, I am not!' Peter replied.

⁵⁹ About an hour later another asserted, 'Certainly this fellow was with him, for he is a Galilean.'

⁶⁰ Peter replied, 'Man, I don't know what you're talking about!' Just as he was speaking, the cock crowed. ⁶¹ The Lord turned and looked straight at Peter. Then Peter remembered the word the Lord had spoken to him: 'Before the cock crows today, you will disown me three times.' ⁶² And he went outside and wept bitterly.

Luke 22:39–62

Jesus places himself directly in God's will. It's a battle for him; he clearly fights against anxiety (vs 42–44). We see the Trinity at work, as the Holy Spirit strengthens Jesus to do his Father's will.

Is there something God is calling you to do, which seems hard?
Are the circumstances surrounding it messy?

Be honest about how you feel and ask the Holy Spirit to empower you to submit to God's authority.

. . . .

. . . .

. . . .

. . . .

. . . .

. . . .

. . . .

. . . .

Day 32

Both Judas and Peter let Jesus down, one by deliberate betrayal, the other through fear and weakness. Have you failed to be faithful? Ask for his forgiveness now.

. . . .

. . . .

. . . .

. . . .

. . . .

. . . .

. . . .

. . . .

. . . .

. . . .

. . . .

. . . .

. . . .

. . . .

. . . .

. . . .

'Holy Spirit, fill me with God's strength to be obedient to your will. Help me be in awe of God and not of my situation.'

¹³ Pilate called together the chief priests, the rulers and the people, ¹⁴ and said to them, 'You brought me this man as one who was inciting the people to rebellion. I have examined him in your presence and have found no basis for your charges against him. ¹⁵ Neither has Herod, for he sent him back to us; as you can see, he has done nothing to deserve death. ¹⁶ Therefore, I will punish him and then release him.'

¹⁸ But the whole crowd shouted, 'Away with this man! Release Barabbas to us!' ¹⁹ (Barabbas had been thrown into prison for an insurrection in the city, and for murder.)

²⁰ Wanting to release Jesus, Pilate appealed to them again. ²¹ But they kept shouting, 'Crucify him! Crucify him!'

Luke 23:13–21

Day 33

Something deep within us recoils when we hear about injustice: an innocent person sent to prison, while a murderer or rapist gets off on a technicality; the poor accused while the rich and powerful use their influence to escape justice; prejudice and racism distorting the scales of justice.

Why do you think the crowd demanded the death of Jesus and release of Barabbas?

Barabbas went free because an innocent man was punished instead. Imagine yourself in Barabbas' place. Reflect on what he must have felt and thought when the jailer came to his cell, only to find release instead of crucifixion. If you like, write down what might have been going through his mind.

In what ways are we all like Barabbas? In what ways are we like the crowd? What does this mean for you personally?

. . . .

. . . .

. . . .

. . . .

. . . .

. . . .

. . . .

Amazing love, O what sacrifice
The Son of God given for me
My debt he pays, and my death he dies
That I might live, that I might live
(Graham Kendrick, © 1989 Make Way Music)

Jesus' innocence went beyond simply insufficient evidence – he lived a perfect life. Thank him for his life-long goodness, love and compassion.

³² Two other men, both criminals, were also led out with him to be executed. ³³ When they came to the place called the Skull, they crucified him there, along with the criminals – one on his right, the other on his left. ³⁴ Jesus said, 'Father, forgive them, for they do not know what they are doing.' And they divided up his clothes by casting lots.

³⁵ The people stood watching, and the rulers even sneered at him. They said, 'He saved others; let him save himself if he is God's Messiah, the Chosen One.'

³⁶ The soldiers also came up and mocked him. They offered him wine vinegar ³⁷ and said, 'If you are the king of the Jews, save yourself.'

³⁸ There was a written notice above him, which read: THIS IS THE KING OF THE JEWS.

³⁹ One of the criminals who hung there hurled insults at him: 'Aren't you the Messiah? Save yourself and us!'

⁴⁰ But the other criminal rebuked him. 'Don't you fear God,' he said, 'since you are under the same sentence? ⁴¹ We are punished justly, for we are getting what our deeds deserve. But this man has done nothing wrong.'

⁴² Then he said, 'Jesus, remember me when you come into your kingdom.'

⁴³ Jesus answered him, 'Truly I tell you, today you will be with me in paradise.'

Luke 23:32–43

What sort of king do Christians worship? What kind of rescuer do we place our faith in? The strange, unsettling truth is that we follow a crucified Messiah, a King who came into his kingdom by dying a shameful death.

This

is

THE KING

of

the

Jews

Jesus forgave even his executioners (v 34). Is there anyone you are struggling to forgive?

Thank Jesus for the forgiveness he has shown you, and ask him to help you forgive others.

Day 34

Of the criminals on the cross, it has been said, 'Do not despair; one of the thieves was saved. Do not presume; one of the thieves was damned.'

How are you tempted to despair of God's grace, or to presume on it?

. . . .

. . . .

. . . .

. . . .

. . . .

. . . .

. . . .

Worship Jesus for his upside-down kingship, dying on a cross to rescue and forgive his enemies – to rescue and forgive you.

⁴⁴ It was now about noon, and darkness came over the whole land until three in the afternoon, ⁴⁵ for the sun stopped shining. And the curtain of the temple was torn in two. ⁴⁶ Jesus called out with a loud voice, 'Father, into your hands I commit my spirit.' When he had said this, he breathed his last.

⁴⁷ The centurion, seeing what had happened, praised God and said, 'Surely this was a righteous man.' ⁴⁸ When all the people who had gathered to witness this sight saw what took place, they beat their breasts and went away. ⁴⁹ But all those who knew him, including the women who had followed him from Galilee, stood at a distance, watching these things.

Luke 23:44–49

Day 35

Darkness, as the Son of God hung dying on a cross.

Put yourself in the shoes of Jesus' followers.
What might they have been thinking and feeling as they watched Jesus die?

There are times when all hope seems lost, when evil appears to have won, when suffering and injustice are overwhelming. At such times, being told that God has a good purpose in it can seem glib and insensitive. How can you hold on to the truth that 'in all things God works for the good of those who love him' (Romans 8:28) while being real about evil and suffering, and sensitive to those who are grieving?

. . . .

. . . .

. . . .

. . . .

. . . .

. . . .

. . . .

. . . .

Lift up situations of darkness to God in prayer. Ask him to shine his light into them, and thank him that Jesus stepped into the darkness for us.

[19] Therefore, brothers and sisters, since we have confidence to enter the Most Holy Place by the blood of Jesus, [20] by a new and living way opened for us through the curtain, that is, his body, [21] and since we have a great priest over the house of God, [22] let us draw near to God with a sincere heart and with the full assurance that faith brings…

Hebrews 10:19–22a

The curtain has been torn in two (v 45)!

Draw near to God through Christ now in thanks and praise.

¹ On the first day of the week, very early in the morning, the women took the spices they had prepared and went to the tomb. ² They found the stone rolled away from the tomb, ³ but when they entered, they did not find the body of the Lord Jesus. ⁴ While they were wondering about this, suddenly two men in clothes that gleamed like lightning stood beside them. ⁵ In their fright the women bowed down with their faces to the ground, but the men said to them, 'Why do you look for the living among the dead? ⁶ He is not here; he has risen! Remember how he told you, while he was still with you in Galilee: ⁷ "The Son of Man must be delivered over to the hands of sinners, be crucified and on the third day be raised again."' ⁸ Then they remembered his words.

Luke 24:1–8

Two men (described by Luke) prompt the women to remember Jesus' words about his resurrection (v 6). Their message reminds them that Jesus' death is not the end. Imagine the mixture of emotions felt by the women after the crucifixion – yet now it is their role to proclaim to the disciples that Jesus lives!

Take a moment to absorb the fact that Jesus has victory over death.
Why does Jesus' resurrection mean hope and good news for the world?

. . . .

. . . .

. . . .

. . . .

. . . .

. . . .

. . . .

. . . .

. . . .

. . . .

Day 36

Praise God that we can live in relationship with God, in fullness of renewed life, through Christ Jesus! (1 Peter 1:21–23).

'Thank you, God, that Jesus' death was your plan
and that I have hope in you, through his resurrection.'

¹³ Now that same day two of them were going to a village called Emmaus, about seven miles from Jerusalem. ¹⁴ They were talking with each other about everything that had happened. ¹⁵ As they talked and discussed these things with each other, Jesus himself came up and walked along with them; ¹⁶ but they were kept from recognising him.

¹⁷ He asked them, 'What are you discussing together as you walk along?'

They stood still, their faces downcast. ¹⁸ One of them, named Cleopas, asked him, 'Are you the only one visiting Jerusalem who does not know the things that have happened there in these days?'

¹⁹ 'What things?' he asked.

'About Jesus of Nazareth,' they replied. 'He was a prophet, powerful in word and deed before God and all the people. ²⁰ The chief priests and our rulers handed him over to be sentenced to death, and they crucified him; ²¹ but we had hoped that he was the one who was going to redeem Israel. And what is more, it is the third day since all this took place. ²² In addition, some of our women amazed us. They went to the tomb early this morning ²³ but didn't find his body. They came and told us that they had seen a vision of angels, who said he was alive. ²⁴ Then some of our companions went to the tomb and found it just as the women had said, but they did not see Jesus.'

²⁵ He said to them, 'How foolish you are, and how slow to believe all that the prophets have spoken! ²⁶ Did not the Messiah have to suffer these things and then enter his glory?' ²⁷ And beginning with Moses and all the Prophets, he explained to them what was said in all the Scriptures concerning himself.

Luke 24:13–27

Day 37

Jesus' friends were in the same place as many people today – uncertain, confused, plagued with doubt. Jesus' crucifixion seemed like a defeat (vs 20,21); they didn't know what to make of the women's story (v 22) or the empty tomb (v 24).

Could Jesus' body have been stolen? What should they make of it?

. . . .

. . . .

. . . .

. . . .

. . . .

. . . .

. . . .

. . . .

. . . .

. . . .

. . . .

. . . .

. . . .

. . . .

. . . .

Why do you think Jesus hid who he was at this point? Are there times when we fail to recognise Jesus' voice, even missing what he is saying to us in the Scriptures?

. . . .

. . . .

. . . .

. . . .

. . . .

. . . .

. . . .

. . . .

Why did Jesus have to first suffer and then enter his glory (v 26)? Thank him that he was willing to suffer the cross for us, and worship him for his glory now.

'Open my mind, Lord Jesus, that I may understand the Scriptures.'

²⁸ As they approached the village to which they were going, Jesus continued on as if he were going further. ²⁹ But they urged him strongly, 'Stay with us, for it is nearly evening; the day is almost over.' So he went in to stay with them.
³⁰ When he was at the table with them, he took bread, gave thanks, broke it and began to give it to them.
³¹ Then their eyes were opened and they recognised him, and he disappeared from their sight. ³² They asked each other, 'Were not our hearts burning within us while he talked with us on the road and opened the Scriptures to us?'
³³ They got up and returned at once to Jerusalem. There they found the Eleven and those with them, assembled together ³⁴ and saying, 'It is true! The Lord has risen and has appeared to Simon.' ³⁵ Then the two told what had happened on the way, and how Jesus was recognised by them when he broke the bread.

Luke 24:28–35

'Lord Jesus, open my eyes to see you as you really are.'

Have you ever had moments of sudden spiritual insight, where God made something clear to you? What happened?

. . . .

. . . .

. . . .

. . . .

. . . .

. . . .

. . . .

. . . .

. . . .

Day 38

Who do you know who is still blind to who Jesus is? Pray for opportunities to open the Scriptures to them, and pray God will open their eyes.

**'Here I am! I stand at the door and knock.
If anyone hears my voice and opens the door,
I will come in and eat with that person, and they with me.'**
Revelation 3:20

Rejoice that we can have fellowship with God through his Son Jesus.
Spend time enjoying his presence now.

36 While they were still talking about this, Jesus himself stood among them and said to them, 'Peace be with you.' 37 They were startled and frightened, thinking they saw a ghost. 38 He said to them, 'Why are you troubled, and why do doubts rise in your minds? 39 Look at my hands and my feet. It is I myself! Touch me and see; a ghost does not have flesh and bones, as you see I have.' 40 When he had said this, he showed them his hands and feet. 41 And while they still did not believe it because of joy and amazement, he asked them, 'Do you have anything here to eat?' 42 They gave him a piece of broiled fish, 43 and he took it and ate it in their presence.

Luke 24:36–43

Day 39

The disciples were just as sceptical as most people today. They wanted physical proof that Jesus was alive. But then they struggled to accept the evidence, because it was so extraordinary – and they were the ones who'd followed Jesus throughout his ministry! Even hearing (v 36), seeing and touching Jesus (v 39) wasn't enough for them. However, it was the down-to-earth physical act of eating that proved to be the pivotal evidence to them that Jesus was no ghost or hallucination. One moment the fish was there in the room, the next it disappeared into Jesus' mouth.

> '... in your hearts revere Christ as Lord.
> **Always be prepared to give an answer to everyone who**
> **asks you to give the reason for the hope that you have.'**
> 1 Peter 3:15

How can you better equip yourself to share the evidence that Jesus really rose from the dead as a fact of history? Ask God to help you grow in knowledge and confidence.

Imagine being in the room as one of the disciples and seeing your friend who had been dead, now alive. Meditate on Christ's words: 'Peace be with you.'

Lift your doubts and troubles to the risen Christ. Let his peace rest on you.

. . . .

. . . .

. . . .

. . . .

. . . .

. . . .

. . . .

. . . .

. . . .

⁴⁴ He said to them, 'This is what I told you while I was still with you: everything must be fulfilled that is written about me in the Law of Moses, the Prophets and the Psalms.'

⁴⁵ Then he opened their minds so they could understand the Scriptures. ⁴⁶ He told them, 'This is what is written: the Messiah will suffer and rise from the dead on the third day, ⁴⁷ and repentance for the forgiveness of sins will be preached in his name to all nations, beginning at Jerusalem. ⁴⁸ You are witnesses of these things. ⁴⁹ I am going to send you what my Father has promised; but stay in the city until you have been clothed with power from on high.'

⁵⁰ When he had led them out to the vicinity of Bethany, he lifted up his hands and blessed them. ⁵¹ While he was blessing them, he left them and was taken up into heaven. ⁵² Then they worshipped him and returned to Jerusalem with great joy. ⁵³ And they stayed continually at the temple, praising God.

Luke 24:44–53

'Lord Jesus, you are the risen one.
Clothe me with the power to be your witness today.'

Jesus' message (vs 46,47) was not for the disciples alone but for the many millions of people who have lived since then. People today need to make a decision about Jesus based on the evidence of these first eyewitnesses. But how can they make a decision unless they are aware of the evidence? And how will they hear of the evidence if they don't have or never open a Bible?

Maybe today is the day you can bring the details of Luke 24 into conversations with colleagues and friends as a disciple called to embody Christ in the world.

Day 40

Are there any parts of the world that God has particularly put on your heart?
Pray for them now.

How can you play your part in sharing the good news with all nations?

Ask the Lord to prepare you to be his messenger and to open the minds of the people
you meet and talk to today.

Notes

Notes

Notes